A COMPLIMENTARY REVIEW COPY, FALL 1968

AN AMERICANS ALL BOOK

William C. Handy: Father of the Blues

BY ELIZABETH RIDER MONTGOMERY
ILLUSTRATED BY DAVID HODGES

ABOUT THE BOOK: A versatile author writes with candor about a great musician in this biography of William C. Handy. Although not the originator of Negro blues music, Handy made an important contribution to American culture as the arranger who wrote the music down and thereby gave it to his country. This book is part of Garrard's new *AMERICANS ALL* series, which will feature inspiring biographies of persons of all nationalities, races, and creeds who have contributed in a specific field to the American way of life.

Subject classification: American Music, Biography
Sub-classification: Blues Music, Reading, Information

ABOUT THE AUTHOR: Elizabeth Rider Montgomery is a versatile author, having written fiction, nonfiction, textbooks, and plays. Most of her work is in the juvenile field, ranging from kindergarten through high school age. She has also contributed many articles and stories to children's magazines. This is one of eight books she has written for Garrard, six of which have been biographies.

Reading Level: Grade 4	Interest Level: Grades 3–6
96 pages . . . 6½ x 9	Publisher's Price: $2.39

Illustrated with photographs and 2-color art; full-color lithographed cover; reinforced binding

GARRARD PUBLISHING COMPANY

Americans All biographies are inspiring life stories about people of all races, creeds, and nationalities who have uniquely contributed to the American way of life. Highlights from each person's story develop his contributions in his special field — whether they be in the arts, industry, human rights, education, science and medicine, or sports.

Specific abilities, character, and accomplishments are emphasized. Often despite great odds, these famous people have attained success in their fields through the good use of ability, determination, and hard work. These fast-moving stories of real people will show the way to better understanding of the ingredients necessary for personal success.

William C. Handy

FATHER
OF THE BLUES

BY ELIZABETH RIDER MONTGOMERY

illustrated by David Hodges

GARRARD PUBLISHING COMPANY
CHAMPAIGN, ILLINOIS

For Jennel Phillips

Picture credits:

Contents

1. A Sinful Instrument

William Christopher Handy entered the log cabin on Handy's Hill where he had lived all his life. Father sat at the kitchen table, reading the Bible. Mother stood on the dirt floor, cooking. Something smelled delicious. William was sure that his mother was the best cook in Florence, Alabama.

It was 1885, and William Handy was

twelve years old. He was born, his father always said, "eight years after surrender." That meant the end of the Civil War, the end of slavery. William had heard many stories about slavery. Grandfather Handy had run away but was soon re-captured. Uncle Hanson, who would not allow anyone to whip him, had been sold into Arkansas and was never heard from again.

As William entered the neat kitchen, his father, a minister in the African Methodist Church, looked up.

"Did you get paid, Sonny?" he asked.

"Yes, sir," the boy replied. His various odd jobs brought in almost three dollars a week.

Father held out his hand. William counted money into it, but closed his own hand on the last few coins.

8

Father smiled. "That goes in your savings, does it?"

"Yes, sir."

"You must have a right good sum by now," Father remarked.

Mother spoke up quickly. "Don't forget, Charles," she said, "William has bought all of his own clothes, books, and school supplies for years."

"William is a good worker," Father agreed, "and I'm glad of it. The devil finds work for idle hands."

The Handy family always had enough to eat. However, if the boy wanted money, he had to earn it. From the age of five, William had earned each week a nickel for Sunday School and a dime for the church collection.

Nobody knew where William kept his money, or what he planned to do with it.

William had always enjoyed music. He loved the spirituals sung in his father's church. He loved the music he was taught in school. He often made music himself by humming through a fine-toothed comb, and he made drums of his mother's tin pans and milk pails. Some day, he vowed, he would have a real musical instrument.

10

For many months he had been saving to buy a guitar. To earn money for it, he had picked berries, fruit, and cotton. He had made lye soap from wood ashes and bones and peddled it from door to door. He had worked as a water boy in the rock quarry for 50 cents a day. Now he had a job as janitor at the courthouse.

William knew the guitar he was going to buy. Every day he stopped on his way home from school and looked at it in the store window. It was a beauty!

Secretly, William counted his money. He had almost enough. Next week he could buy the guitar!

The days dragged past. At last he was paid again. Home he ran for the rest of his money, then back to the store.

"I want to buy that guitar," William told the clerk.

The clerk named the price, certain that the boy did not have that much cash. But William only nodded. He laid a cloth bundle on the counter and untied it.

"That's exactly what I have," he said. He began to count out the money. The clerk's eyes grew wide. What a heap of small coins!

William added the last penny to the pile. "There," he said with his friendly smile. "May I have my guitar, please?"

The amazed clerk handed him the beautiful instrument. William walked out, so happy he could scarcely breathe.

When he reached home, he hurried along the flower-bordered path. His parents were in the kitchen. William held out the guitar and waited for their admiring comments. For a long moment nobody made a sound.

12

"It's my guitar," William said at last. "I saved the money and bought it."

Then Father stood up. He pointed an accusing finger at the shining instrument.

"You bought a guitar!" he gasped. "Why, that's a devil's plaything!"

Astonished, William drew the guitar back. His mother saw his bewilderment. She explained that his father considered all music sinful, except church music. William had heard that, but had never believed it.

"Take it away!" Father shouted. "How could you bring such a sinful instrument into this house?"

"I want to be a musician," William said.

His father was furious. "My son a musician! I will never permit it, never! You're going to be a minister of the gospel like me!"

14

William hugged the precious guitar.

"Take it back!" Father ordered. "Get that big dictionary in the store window. That will help you with your studies."

William did take it back and exchanged it for a dictionary. But he never looked up a word in the dictionary after that without thinking of the guitar he couldn't keep.

2. The Side-Valve Cornet

One fine spring day William stood up for the daily singing lesson with the rest of the students in the Florence District School for Negroes. He was now fifteen and twice as tall as the primary grade pupils.

Professor Wallace blew a note on his pitch pipe, and each student hummed his own starting pitch.

The professor led the singing choir in the "Soldiers' Chorus" from *Faust*. First they sang it with "sol-fa" syllables. Then they sang the words. They had no musical accompaniment, for there was no piano or organ in the ungraded school.

This was the hour of the day William liked best. For nine years he had had the same teacher, with daily lessons in part-singing and in reading music. All the sounds of the outdoors had become music to William. Each bird sang its own combination of notes. Each animal seemed to play a musical instrument. The blue jay had a French horn, the bullfrog a bass fiddle, the woodpecker a snare drum, and the whippoorwill a clarinet.

William interpreted other sounds in musical terms, too. The whistle of one steamboat on the nearby Tennessee River sang "do-sol," while another sang "do-mi." A galloping horse had one rhythm, and a trotting horse a different one.

When Professor Wallace put away his pitch pipe, the school settled down to study geography.

William was a good student and enjoyed school. But today he stared unseeingly at his geography book. It was a fine day to play baseball, but a painful blow in the eye by a ball had dulled William's fondness for the game. Nothing, however, could quench the boy's love for music.

Through the open schoolhouse window William heard a plowman singing:

Aye-o, aye-o,
I wouldn't live in Cairo.

The man sang the simple song over and over. In his mind William put the correct musical syllables to the tune.

18

Idly he wondered why the singer wouldn't live in Cairo.

Then William began to tap out tunes on his desk. He was practicing the fingering of a cornet, yet he had never had a cornet in his hands.

Although his father had made him return the guitar, he was still determined to get a musical instrument. He was learning to play one, but nobody knew

it, not even the man who was teaching him.

A circus band had become stranded in Florence, and the bandmaster had started teaching a Negro band. The lessons were conducted in a barber shop with a big window.

Every day, on his way home from school, William stopped in front of the barber shop. He had chosen the cornet, a type of trumpet, as his instrument, so he watched the cornetist closely. He also studied the chart on the blackboard that illustrated cornet fingering.

Day after day he watched and memorized. Day after day he fingered scales and tunes on his school desk. He was careful not to get caught, because Professor Wallace was as strongly opposed to band music as his father.

Somehow one of the band members, Will Bates, learned what the boy was doing. The next time he watched outside the barber shop, Bates went out to talk to him.

"How would you like to buy my old cornet?" he asked. "I'm getting a new one."

William's brown eyes shone. He looked at the dingy, battered brass horn as if it were solid gold. It was an old-fashioned instrument, with side-valves operated by catgut strings. To William it seemed a treasure beyond price.

"How much?" he asked.

"I'll sell it to you for $1.75," Bates offered.

"All I've got right now is a quarter," William answered. "But I can pay more money later."

Bates held out the horn. "Give me your two bits, boy, and pay two bits a week."

The deal was made, and now William was the proud possessor of a side-valve cornet. He couldn't take it home, because Father wouldn't have it in the house. He couldn't take the horn to school, because Professor Wallace would seize it. But he

found a secret hiding place, and he practiced daily until he could play quite well.

Soon William Handy began to play with the Florence band. He was also asked to sing tenor in a quartet. Every time the band got an engagement, he went along. He was happier than he had ever been in his life, because he was now making music. Somehow neither his father nor his teacher learned what he was doing.

Then one day the band was asked to play at a land sale, several miles away. If William went with them, he would have to skip school. Then his father and his teacher would certainly find out about his music. But he decided to go anyway. Surely Father would forgive him when he gave him eight dollars, his pay for one day's playing.

William Handy discovered that he did not know his father very well, after all. Father was furious that his son was taking money for making music.

"That is sinful!" Father shouted. "I will never forgive you, William! Never!"

This time William was not swayed by his father's anger. He had no intention of giving up either his instrument or his band work. Even when Professor Wallace whipped him for skipping school, and again for playing the cornet, he did not change his mind. Making music was something that William Handy just had to do.

3. Singing for His Supper

Throughout the rest of his school days in Florence, William played with the band and sang with the quartet. William studied hard too. He was graduated near the head of his class. Then he left home, hoping to earn enough money to attend college. He hated to say good-bye to his mother and father and his baby brother Charles, but he was determined to go to a larger city.

On September 7, 1892, William went to Birmingham, planning to teach school. However, he got a better-paying job in the steel furnaces of nearby Bessemer at $1.85 a day.

Although working over blinding molten metal hurt his eyes, William enjoyed Bessemer. He organized a brass band. He got a job leading a small orchestra and teaching the members to read music. He played trumpet with a church choir and began to save money for college.

Then everything changed. A panic, or depression, set in. Many factories and mills shut down or cut down. William's pay was reduced to 90 cents a day. Even this was not real money but merely paper "scrip," good only at the company store. So William quit his job and returned to Birmingham.

In a short time his college money was gone and he was penniless. William walked the streets aimlessly.

One evening he heard some young men singing. He asked them, "Can you sing 'Gwine Chop 'Em in the Head With a Golden Axe?'"

The singers shook their heads.

"I can teach it to you," William said. And he began to sing:

Hear dat trumpet sound.
Stand up and don't fall down.
Slip and slide around
Till your shoes don't have no tacks . . . .

He organized the boys into a quartet and taught them to read music. They called themselves the Lauzetta Quartet.

William's quartet became popular in

28

Birmingham, but the boys made little money because everybody was poor. So William suggested that they go to the World's Fair in Chicago.

"People from all over the country would hear us there," he said. "We'd become famous."

"That's a great idea," said one of the singers. "But how would we get to Chicago? I haven't a dime."

"Neither have I," said the other boys.

William turned his pockets inside out. He had only 20 cents. "What does money matter?" he said with a cheerful smile. "We'll ride a freight train to Chicago. Then we can make our way by singing."

One day in 1893 the four boys met at the railroad tracks and hopped a freight. When the train stopped at a station, however, the brakeman put them off.

"If you get on again," he threatened, "I'll kick you off while the train is moving."

Four unhappy boys stood beside the railroad tracks and watched the train prepare to move on. Negroes were not welcome in this town, they knew. What should they do?

Rich or poor, happy or sad, there was one thing that 19-year-old William Handy could always do. He leaned his head toward his companions and hummed the starting pitch for their favorite song, "When the Summer Breeze Was Blowing."

As the brakeman began to raise his lantern in his signal to the engineer, sweet harmony reached his ears. At once he lowered the lantern and called to the boys.

"I didn't know you boys could sing,"

he shouted. "Get back on the train. You can ride in the caboose with me."

When they reached Chicago, the boys were disappointed. Nobody was interested in their singing. So they hopped a freight train for St. Louis. Again they were disappointed. That city, too, was suffering from a depression. The boys couldn't even get jobs on the levee, the high bank that kept the Mississippi River from overflowing. At last the Lauzetta Quartet disbanded. Each boy went his own way.

For the very first time, William Handy learned what hard times were. He considered himself lucky now when he had even a crust of bread to eat, and when he could sleep in a stable with horses. Often he slept in vacant lots and even on the cobblestones of the Mississippi

levee. How hard those stones were!

And then, as if hunger and homeless-
ness were not enough, William's clothes
became infested with lice. Wearing only a
threadbare coat and pants, he tossed his
shirt and underwear into the river.

Unshaven, lonely, and poor, he walked
the streets of St. Louis. He could go
back home, he knew. But he would have
to give up music and become a minister.

As he passed a "white" saloon, he heard a man singing to the music of a guitar. After a moment's hesitation, he went inside, although he knew he might be thrown out. He asked for a chance to show what he could do. Strumming the borrowed guitar, he began to sing:

Sometimes my heart grows weary
    of its sadness,
Sometimes my life grows weary
    of its pain.

The crowd loved William's singing and asked for more. Then somebody took up a collection for him. By the time the place closed, William had enough money to buy new clothes. Now he was sure he would not go home. Somehow he would make his way with music.

4. Minstrel Man

William drifted on from St. Louis. Occasionally he got a few days' work at paving streets or digging ditches. Usually his singing ability rather than his limited physical strength got him the job. Negro work gangs always sang at their labor. The song set the rhythm for the hammers, the shovels, or the picks. The more the men sang, the better they worked.

William heard Negroes sing about their joys and their sorrows. A Negro sang

36

one song when he was happy, and another when he was sad, but always he sang. Although William felt the only important music was found in books, he listened to these "earth-born" melodies and stored them away in his memory.

In his drifting William stopped in Evansville, Indiana. Soon he was playing with the Hampton Cornet Band and with another band in Henderson, Kentucky, just across the river. He was beginning to be recognized as a fine musician.

William worked for a time, too, as janitor in the rehearsal hall of the Henderson Singing Society. In this way he could hear good music while earning money.

Two important things happened to William in Henderson, Kentucky. First, he met a girl whom he wanted to marry. And then in August of 1896, he received an important letter. A friend who was with Mahara's Minstrels wanted him to come to Chicago and try out for the troupe. The minstrel show of that time was the forerunner of today's musical comedy.

William showed the letter to his girl, Elizabeth Price.

"It's a fine chance," he said. "The salary is six dollars a week, plus 'cakes', or meals. When times get better, we could get married."

But Elizabeth did not share William's enthusiasm. "You know what my folks think of minstrels," she said.

William nodded. "They think minstrels are a pretty low crowd. But is there any other way for Negro musicians to get started?"

"Stay in Henderson, William" Elizabeth urged, "and go into the grocery business."

William, with cornet in hand, poses in the uniform of the Hampton Cornet Band.

William had no intention of going into the grocery business in Henderson or anywhere else. In spite of Elizabeth's disapproval, he went to Chicago and joined Mahara's Minstrels.

Immediately, luck began to smile. The bass violin player quit and William took his post, although he had never had lessons on the bass fiddle. His salary was raised to seven dollars a week.

Soon somebody said the show ought to have a really good quartet, so William trained one. Again his salary was raised. He bought a brand new gold-plated trumpet, he practiced hard every day, and he was given a part in the show as a cornet soloist. Again his salary took a sharp upswing.

William bought some fine clothes. He began to grow a moustache. He looked very elegant and handsome now. But his friendly smile was his chief attraction.

Mahara's Minstrels were managed by three Irish brothers, William, Jack and Frank Mahara. The company traveled in its own Pullman car. Usually it played in a different town each night.

A minstrel man's day began at 11:45 A.M. The parade manager blew his whistle, and the parade began to form. It was just like a circus parade of those days. First the Maharas, wearing high silk hats and fine suits, rode by in their four-horse carriage. They smiled and bowed to the crowds. Next came another carriage with the stars of the show. Comedians, singers, and acrobats followed on foot. The band marched behind them, led by a strutting drum major. Boys carried big banners.

As the procession paraded through the town, the band played lively marches. When it reached the public square, the parade halted. Townspeople gathered around, and the band played a concert of classical and popular music. Then the company paraded back to the theater.

The musicians had the remainder of the afternoon free, but they must be on hand promptly at 7:30 for the evening performance. It would be long past midnight before they got to bed. While they slept, the train would take them to another town, where the whole routine would be repeated the next day.

The following season the Mahara brothers decided to carry two bands with their show. They offered the leadership of one band to William C. Handy.

Jubilantly William wrote to Elizabeth

Price. He would lead a band of 30 instruments in the daily parades and 42 instruments in the nightly concerts. He would wear a handsome uniform, with gold epaulettes on the shoulders, and a shiny high silk hat. His salary would be in keeping with his position. Now, he told Elizabeth, they could get married. But she was still reluctant to marry a minstrel man.

Life for William Handy had become a series of one-night stands. From Florida to California Mahara's Minstrels traveled. They played from Seattle to New York and from Canada to Mexico. William saw almost every state that he had heard about in geography lessons. He met fine people, and he met evil people.

One day William had a close call. During the noon concert in a Texas town, he was playing a cornet solo. Suddenly, he noticed that a rifle was pointed at his eye. Hiding his fear, he kept on playing.

The concert ended at last, and the rifle had not been fired. The band fell into marching formation for the parade to the theater. Then out of the crowd rode a gang of cowboys with lassos.

"Yippe-i-ee!" screeched the cowboys, twirling their ropes. They let them fly at the marching minstrels. A crowd of young hoodlums began to throw rocks.

"Look!" squealed one boy. "My stone fell into the big horn!"

Another boy tossed a handful of rocks on the bass drum.

William Handy had begun to direct the band in a march. But when lassos and rocks continued to fall, he lowered his cornet. He was normally a kind, peaceful person, but injustice infuriated him.

"Do not play!" he snapped. "March!" And he set the pace, marching twice as fast as usual. Still in formation, the band quick-stepped along the street. At last they were safe inside the theater, and their tormentors disappeared.

The Maharas praised William for his conduct. "You handled a difficult situation exactly right," they said. "We're proud of you."

One day Mahara's Minstrels played in Huntsville, Alabama, not far from Handy's home town. His mother had died several years before, and he had not been home since.

During the noon concert, William saw his father in the crowd, and he played as he had never played before.

46

Soon William heard his father speak. "The leader of the band is my son," he was saying to the people around him. "Yes, sir, that's my boy!"

That night Father attended the minstrel show. When the curtain fell, he came up to William and shook his hand.

"Sonny," he said, "this is the first show I have seen in many years. I want you to know that I am proud of you and that I forgive you for becoming a musician."

W.C. Handy, to the left of the drum, led
both band and orchestra at A.&M. College.

5. A Composer Is Born

In July, 1898 William had finally per-suaded Elizabeth to marry him. Some-times she accompanied him on his travels with Mahara's Minstrels, but she hoped he would soon settle down. At last, when their first child Lucile was born, he left the show. For two years he taught music at the Agricultural and Mechanical College for Negroes at Huntsville. Another year with Mahara's Minstrels followed. Later he accepted a position in Clarksdale, Mississippi, directing a Negro Knights of Pythias band.

Handy and his band played up and down the Mississippi River. They were hired for lavish dances at plantation mansions, for country square-dances, for the opening of new parks and new stores. They were hired to play on excursion boats and at parades, barbecues, fairs, and political rallies.

One night, Handy and his band were playing for a dance in Cleveland, Mississippi. A note was handed to him:

"Would you play some Negro music?"

The request puzzled Handy. His carefully trained musicians could not play without musical scores. He gave the cue for a Stephen Foster melody.

Soon a second note was passed to Handy:

"Would you object if a local Negro band played a few dances?"

50

Delighted to have a rest, his band filed off the platform. They were replaced by a bedraggled trio carrying a shabby guitar, a mandolin, and a bass fiddle.

When the newcomers began to play, Handy thought their music rather dreadful. It was so monotonous! Then he began to realize that it might be monotonous, but it was far from unpleasant. It was a haunting sort of tune that you

could not forget. He wondered whether people at the dance would care for it.

The answer was "yes." The people swayed and stamped as they danced. Moreover, they showered money at the feet of the players—quarters, half dollars, and silver dollars. Handy's eyes widened. Those untrained musicians were getting more money for playing one dance than his men were paid for the entire evening!

William Christopher Handy's idea of music changed completely that night. At last he could see the value of the Negro folk music he had been listening to all his life.

The next day Handy wrote musical scores for several folk tunes. After that he included them on the program whenever he played for dances. The effect was astonishing. People danced as they had danced to the music of the ragged string band in Cleveland, Mississippi, and they showered coins on the musicians.

From that time on, Handy's band often played the "blues," as this kind of music came to be known. Their popularity quickly doubled.

Soon, in addition to his Clarksdale work, Handy took on a Knights of Pythias band in Memphis, Tennessee. He made it into a dance orchestra, one of the first in the country to include a saxophone.

Twice a week Handy traveled on the train 76 miles to Memphis for rehearsals. He carried his cornet, saxophone, violin, typewriter, and suitcase. As the train lurched along, Handy wrote letters and arranged musical scores. This was very hard on his eyes, but it saved time. Time was most precious, now that he was working in two cities.

In 1909 a political campaign became the center of attention in Memphis. Three candidates were running for the office of mayor. Each political group hired a band to advertise its candidate. Handy's band was hired by the campaign manager for Edward H. Crump, the reform candidate.

As Handy racked his brain for good campaign music, a tune started running through his head. It was a weird melody, based on the "sorrow songs" he had heard all his life. Quickly he wrote it down.

The tune was unusual in form. Most popular songs are written in four-line stanzas, with sixteen measures of music. But Handy wrote his new tune in the form of Negro folk songs, which have three-line stanzas, with only twelve measures of music.

The melody itself was as unusual as the form. Like the songs of Negro workmen, Handy's new tune had both sadness and joy, with swooping, slurring notes.

The rhythm was different too. The strong beat came, not on the first beat of the measure, but on the after-beat. All in all, it was a haunting, attention-getting piece.

Handy's musicians loved the new tune. On the appointed day they arrived at Main and Madison Streets ready to play.

A bandwagon had been decorated with gaudy banners. In the wagon were chairs for the band and their instruments, which included a violin, guitar, string bass, clarinet, saxophone, and trombone. Handy himself played the trumpet.

The horses began to pull the wagon along the street. Handy tapped his feet, then gave the signal to play. By the time the band had played the first twelve measures, people were dancing on the sidewalks and even in the street. When the music stopped, everybody shouted, "More! More! Play it again."

A man stepped directly in front of the horses. "What's the name of that tune?" he asked.

The guitar player pointed to Mr. Crump's banner on the wagon. "It's 'Mr. Crump,'" he said. "That's what it is."

As the band repeated "Mr. Crump," people along the street sang in tune with it. Some laughed at the candidate, some joked about his proposed reforms. But all were noticing Mr. Crump's name. Whether Handy's music had anything to do with it or not, Edward Crump won the election for mayor of Memphis.

Handy's new tune was finished as a campaign song, but it continued to be popular. Handy was swamped with calls to play for dances. He divided his orchestra into three groups, and each was kept busy. Still, they could not keep up with the demand. So Handy hired more players, and still more. Finally he had on his payroll 67 musicians, divided into a dozen bands. All reported that "Mr. Crump" was their most popular tune.

Handy wanted to publish it. But, one after another, music publishers turned it down.

Nearly three years passed. W.C. Handy moved his growing family to Memphis.

Finally he decided to publish "Mr. Crump" himself, under the title of "Memphis Blues." An acquaintance, man-

An early photo of W.C. Handy listening to
the first recording of "Memphis Blues"

ager of the music section of a department store, offered to take care of the business details, and Handy agreed to pay for a first printing of 1,000 copies.

On Friday afternoon, September 27, 1912, the sheet music of "Memphis Blues" arrived. When Handy opened the package and saw 1,000 blue-covered copies of his song, he was thrilled.

As the days passed, however, the thrill faded. The tune did not sell, Handy was told. He could not understand why, because Memphis had been dancing to that music for almost three years. Yet the music manager showed him a big stack of unsold copies.

At last, discouraged, W.C. Handy sold his rights to "Memphis Blues" for $50. He received back almost 1,000 copies. Since he had paid for a printing of 1,000,

Handy believed that was all the remaining sheet music.

Later, Handy learned that he had been cheated. The music manager had had 2,000 copies printed. Thus he could sell 1,000 and still show the composer a stack of unsold music to prove that people wouldn't buy it.

"Memphis Blues" soon became a great hit. The Victor Company made a recording of it. Everywhere he went, W.C. Handy heard his tune played and sung, but he didn't make a cent from it.

6. "St. Louis Blues"

At first Handy was bitter about being cheated. But he soon decided not to waste time or energy on resentment. Instead, he wrote another tune, called "Jogo Blues." Then he had a talk with his friend, Harry A. Pace.

"I learned something from my experience with 'Memphis Blues,'" Handy said. "I learned that my music will sell."

"Certainly it will sell," Pace agreed. "Your songs will make money."

"I don't want to make money for somebody else," the composer said.

"Publish your own music, then, W.C.," said Pace. Handy's friends had begun to call him "W.C."

"I've been thinking about that, Harry," Handy replied. "But I need a partner."

The two men exchanged thoughtful glances. They had known each other six years, and they had much in common. Although Pace was a bank cashier and did not make a living from music, he had a fine singing voice, a deep interest in music, and he wrote good song lyrics. The two men had become friends. They collaborated on song-writing, Pace doing the lyrics and Handy, the music. Their first song, "In the Cotton Fields of Dixie," had been published by a Cincinnati firm.

Now Pace knew what was in Handy's mind. After a moment he nodded. "Yes, W.C., I'll go in business with you."

So the firm of "Pace and Handy, Music Publishers" was formed. The first songs it published were Handy's "Jogo Blues" and Pace's "The Girl You Never Have Met."

"Jogo Blues" was not a hit. Handy became discouraged and felt himself a failure. He was 40 years old and he had a growing family to support, yet his income averaged only about $2.50 a day.

Soon a new tune began to beat in Handy's head, and he wanted to write it down. Four lively, healthy children made his Memphis home a happy place, but they made concentration difficult. Handy decided to find a place away from home in which to work.

One evening in September, 1913, Handy packed a suitcase and—without telling Elizabeth—he slipped away from the house. He rented a room with a piano in the Beale Street section of Memphis, and there he set to work.

Outside the rented room, the lights flickered. Roustabouts from river boats sauntered along the street, laughing, singing, and shouting, and so did the customary evening crowds. It was a warm night. Through wide-open windows, Handy heard piano music. None of this bothered him, however. He was listening to the music in his head, and he was reliving in memory his months as a drifter at the age of nineteen.

Memories flooded over him. He recalled town after town he had visited where Negroes were warned not to let the sun

go down on them there. He felt again the hard cobblestones of the Mississippi levee under him. He saw himself tossing his lice-ridden clothes into the muddy river. He heard himself singing in a St. Louis saloon and twanging a guitar. Penniless, unshaven, with no clothes under his coat and pants—how miserable he had been!

Handy saw and heard again a woman he had met as he wandered in St. Louis. She was wailing, "Ma man's got a heart like a rock cast in de sea."

Now the "earth-born" melodies that Handy had been storing in his memory all his life came to the surface of his mind. He recalled the long-ago song of the Negro plowman, the songs of many Negro work gangs, the individual "sorrow songs" and "jubilation songs" he had listened to. Bits of them ran together to fuse with the tune in his mind.

The night was passing rapidly, and still Handy had put nothing down on paper. Now he dipped his pen in ink and wrote, "I hate to see de evenin' sun go down."

Once started, the lyrics practically wrote themselves, in the three-line stanza of folk songs:

I hate to see de eve-nin' sun go down,
Hate to see de eve-nin' sun go down,
'Cause my baby, he done lef' dis town.

And then he began to write the music. Handy tossed each sheet of manuscript on the floor as he finished it, so the ink would dry and the notes would not blur. On he worked in the dim lamplight.

The sun had begun to shine through

68

the window of the rented room before Handy completed his new piece. Rubbing his aching eyes, he wrote a title on the manuscript: "St. Louis Blues."

Handy did not take time to go home, nor did he think of sending a message to his wife. He spent the day writing arrangements of "St. Louis Blues" for each member of his main band. That evening, as the band played at the exclusive Alaskan Roof Garden, Handy introduced "St. Louis Blues" to the world.

The song was a hit. At the end of the evening the composer said to his band, "Come on home with me and we'll celebrate our new hit."

When the musicians got out of their cabs in front of Handy's home, they learned that at least one member of the W.C. Handy family had no thought of

celebrating. Elizabeth Handy met them at the door, and she was angry.

"Where have you been?" she asked her husband. "Where have you been for more than 24 hours? I've been worried sick!"

Only then did Handy remember that he had not told his wife one word about his intention of writing a new "blues" song. It took a while to explain his absence satisfactorily. How the musicians laughed to hear their leader apologizing so humbly!

When the band played the new piece for Elizabeth, however, she understood her husband's forgetfulness. She tapped her foot in time with the music and smiled forgivingly at him.

William Christopher Handy had written a very big hit indeed. For the rest of his life, he would be pointed out as the composer of "St. Louis Blues."

7. Success and Failure

Handy published "St. Louis Blues" immediately. Kress and Woolworth had recently installed sheet music departments in their stores all over the country. Handy got enough advance orders from these ten-cent stores to pay the total printing bill for 10,000 copies.

Handy had the entire responsibility for the young publishing firm, because Pace now had a fine job in Georgia. If the company

"Words and music by W.C. Handy"—an early copy of sheet music for "St. Louis Blues"

was to make money, he also had to write music. For hours at a time Handy sat at the piano, tapping his foot as he worked out new tunes.

In addition to writing and publishing music, Handy had a dozen bands to keep busy. The more popular his "blues" became, the busier W.C. Handy was. Fortunately, his young brother Charles came to his rescue. Now a grown man, Charles helped W.C. with the music publishing business. Soon Handy wondered how he had ever managed without him.

Handy's two new "blues" songs, "Beale Street Blues" and "Hooking Cow Blues," were very popular, and he was asked to go to New York and make some records.

In spite of all these successes, W.C. Handy could not build up a respectable bank account. Instead of diminishing, his expenses continually increased. Sometimes Handy even had to pawn his instruments to get money to pay bills.

One Saturday night Handy was leading a band at the Colonial Country Club. As he played his trumpet, he wished the club would hire them for an extra hour, so that they could each earn another dollar.

Toward midnight Handy was called to the telephone. His brother Charles was on the line.

"I stopped at the post office just now," Charles said, "to see if anything had come in the night mail from New York."

"Was there anything?" Handy asked.

"Only a check from the Victor Recording Company on the record of 'Beale Street Blues.'" The Victor check usually ran about $200, but from Charles' tone it might be a bit more this time.

"How much?" asked Handy.

"Guess," said Charles.

"Three hundred?" guessed Handy.

"More."

"Five hundred?"

"You're way too low."

"I give up."

Triumphantly Charles announced, "The check is for $1,857!"

W.C. Handy laughed unsteadily, "And to think I was wishing the Colonial Club would hire us for one more hour so that we could earn an extra dollar apiece!"

When Handy returned to his band, he learned that the club had hired them for *three* more hours!

On Monday morning he received $3,827 from Columbia Records, and the following day $1,000 from the Emerson Company. Pace & Handy had attained success.

The next few years brought many changes, both in the affairs of William Christopher Handy and in America. Telephones and electric lights became very common. There was talk of a brand-new invention called radio. Automobiles became popular. People said they might even replace horses.

In April, 1917, the United States entered World War I. The war changed many things, but there was as much prejudice as ever. Many Negroes fought side by side with other Americans in the trenches in Europe, and President Wilson chose Negro troops to guard the White House. Yet civilian Negroes were often treated most unfairly.

Handy bought United States Defense Bonds. He played without pay for rallies and fund-raising events. Yet when a Preparedness Day parade was held in Memphis, no Negro bands were allowed to take part in it. And when the historic Liberty Bell was brought through Memphis, only white children were permitted to march past it. Negro children, including five young Handys, had to watch from the sidewalk.

Incidents like these helped to make up Handy's mind when Pace suggested that they move to New York. It was time, he thought, to leave the South. He moved his family to New York and opened an office there. Harry came from Atlanta to be president of the company; Charles became vice-president; and W.C., secretary-treasurer.

For a few years the firm of Pace & Handy prospered. The partners sometimes disagreed, but they never quarreled.

Off for a "ride" at Coney Island, New York— the Handys, l. to r., Lucile, W.C., Jr., Elizabeth, W. C., Wyer, Katharine, Mrs. Handy

Then, in the 1920's, almost without warning, trouble came.

Several record companies went bankrupt, owing Pace & Handy a great deal of money. The Woolworth stores closed their 600 music counters, and other ten-cent stores followed their lead. The firm of Pace & Handy was left with more than 300,000 copies of ten-cent music which could not be sold.

Although their income had decreased sharply, the firm's expenses remained as large as ever. There were printing bills and advertising bills. There were wages for the large office staff, the salesmen, and the song-pluggers. The firm of Pace & Handy was in trouble.

Then one sad day, the final blow fell.

"I'm leaving the company, W.C.," Pace told Handy.

"Leaving?" Handy repeated, aghast. "Why?"

"I'm organizing my own firm, the Pace Phonograph Company."

Handy tried to persuade Pace to change his mind. "I know we haven't always agreed, Harry," he said. "But I didn't dream you'd leave the company."

"For a long time, I've wanted to be on my own," Pace replied.

"Don't leave now," Handy begged, "when everything is in such a dreadful state."

Harry Pace shrugged. "Sorry, W.C., but my company is ready to roll."

Pace moved out, taking with him many of their best employees. Handy was left short-handed as well as deeply in debt.

Now Handy did most of the firm's work himself. Often he labored half the

82

night transcribing music. On Sundays he did the bookkeeping. He became completely exhausted.

Through Handy's entire life, his eyes had bothered him. First there was that boyhood baseball injury; then the work over molten metal at Bessemer; and finally, years of writing music by the inadequate light of coal-oil lamps or on lurching trains. But in spite of frequent

eye pain, Handy had never once consulted a doctor.

Now the pain became almost unendurable, and his sight faded. He could not see to shave, to read, or to write music. His wife put hot towels on his eyes, but the relief was merely temporary.

Finally, Mrs. Handy persuaded him to call a doctor. "Your husband will lose his sight," the doctor said.

8. Father of the Blues

W.C. Handy sat in the dark in a small apartment. Tears streamed from his tortured eyes. He had sold his home to help pay his debts. Suffering, unable to work, dependent on his family to lead him around, he faced a hopeless future. What was there to live for, if he could neither see music nor write it?

Lawyers advised him to go into bankruptcy. Because Pace & Handy was a corporation, Handy could do this legally. It would mean closing the business and saying he could not pay his debts. Then the people to whom the firm owed money would not get paid.

To Handy, bankruptcy might be legal, but it was not ethical. Even though Handy owned little more than half the company, he wanted to pay all of the firm's debts. Nobody was going to lose anything on his account, Handy vowed, although he didn't know how he could prevent it.

During these dreadful days, one thing cheered him. The worse his pain and financial situation became, the more comfort he found in friendship. Old friends came to the rescue with loans and gifts. New friends stood by him, ready to help. People whom he had helped years before now came forward to pay long-overdue loans. His wife, his brother, and his children all worked to keep the business going.

One day Handy asked his wife to read to him from the Bible. After that, she read to him daily. Handy also turned for comfort to the Negro spirituals he had sung as a boy in his father's church. Following the evening Bible reading, he would sing one spiritual after another. Religion became more meaningful. The assurance of God's love and care began to dispel the blackness of his despair. Again W.C. Handy wanted to live.

"Life is a lot like playing the trumpet," he said. "You've got to blow something into it to get something out. If I get well, I'll try to *live* my religion. I'll spend my life helping others."

Soon Handy began to sit at the piano again and pick out tunes. One red letter day his family woke up to the sound of his trumpet. Handy was playing "St. Louis Blues"! Everybody in the house went around smiling, for they knew W.C. was getting well.

In a short time he was strong enough to undergo an operation on his eyes. His sight returned, although the doctors warned it might fail again.

Finally, Handy was able to return to his office. As business improved, he paid off the company's debts. But all the while he shared his money with young song-writers, singers, actors, and blind people. And the more he helped others, the more his own business prospered.

Many honors came to him, too. A park in Memphis, Tennessee, and a school in

Florence, Alabama, were named for him. St. Louis established a scholarship fund in his honor for young people who had musical talent. His name was included in *Who's Who in America* and *Who's Who in Music*, and placed on a list of 600 foremost contributors to American culture. This was a great honor.

In 1940 Handy took part in a great music festival at the Golden Gate Exposition in San Francisco. He sat in the front row of the big open-air pavilion, with Irving Berlin on one side of him and Shelton Brooks, composer of "Darktown Strutters' Ball," on the other. Handy listened as famous composers played their own music.

"The next performer," announced the master of ceremonies, "will be W.C. Handy, Father of the Blues."

90

Handy walked toward the platform. He gave a few soft toots on his trumpet to see if his lip was in good condition. The orchestra played an eight-bar introduction to "St. Louis Blues," and Handy began to play.

A storm of applause greeted his performance. Deeply touched, W.C. Handy made his way back to his seat. He was humbly thankful for the popularity of his music. He was not so much a composer of the "blues," he knew, as an arranger. Thousands had heard the Negro folk songs, but he was the first to write them down and give them to his country. Now they could be enjoyed by everyone.

"St. Louis Blues" remained Handy's masterpiece. For more than 25 years it was the most popular piece of music in America. Handy's royalties amounted to

In a thoughtful mood, W.C. Handy plays a
few bars of his famous "St. Louis Blues."

$25,000 a year. Its popularity spread all over the world. It was played in palaces and in tumbledown cottages, in night clubs and in opera houses.

The original copyright on "Memphis Blues" expired in 1940, and Handy took over the rights himself. This was a great satisfaction.

Soon Handy's sight began to fail again, and doctors could do nothing to help. By 1945 he had lost the use of his eyes completely. This time he did not despair. He never faltered in his resolution to "live his religion." He continued to share his time, his talent, and his money with others.

In spite of his blindness, Handy kept on working. His mail had to be read to him, and all writing had to be dictated. But he continued to be the moving spirit of Handy Brothers Music Company, as the firm was called now, until he was a very old man.

One day a reporter asked Handy what he would still like to do for his country and its music.

"I'd like to make my country realize," Handy replied, "that the spirit of the Negro is the spirit of America. I'd like to convince my countrymen that we are Americans too."

When Handy was 84, a motion picture entitled "St. Louis Blues" was made of his life. Since he was too ill and weak to attend the theater, the film was brought to his home in Westchester County, New York. Handy could not see the film, of course, but he was delighted with the music and the dialogue.

A few weeks later, on March 28, 1958,

William Christopher Handy closed his sightless eyes forever. At the time, Deems Taylor, noted music critic, said of him: "As the Father of the Blues, he has contributed something to the world's music that is absolutely new and absolutely American." Handy's memory lives on today in the sad and beautiful music he fathered.